HANDBOOK
FOR THE
Recently
Deceased

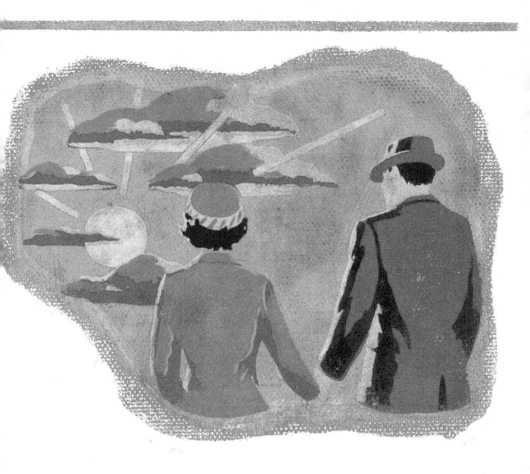

ISBN: 978-1-951161-99-6

Copyright © 2020 by TIMELINE Publishers

Handbook for the Recently Deceased

This Handbook Belongs To

....

....

Welcome to the first day of the
rest of your afterlife.
Not everyone who dies becomes a ghost,
but there are many, many more ghosts
in the world around you than you may
have realized.
You can chalk it up to living-privilege bias;
live people ignore the strange and unusual.
Naturally, functional parameters vary
from manifestation to manifestation.
But as you make your way through
your ethereal existence,
you will no doubt find a style of haunting
that suits your personality,
disposition, and ectoplasmic make-up.

These aren't my rules. Come to think of it, I don't have any rules.

Beetlejuice

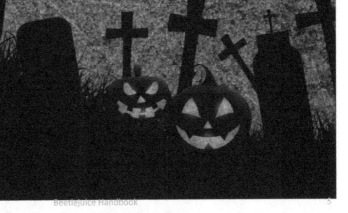

Handbook for the Recently Deceased

Note

Note

Doodle

Note

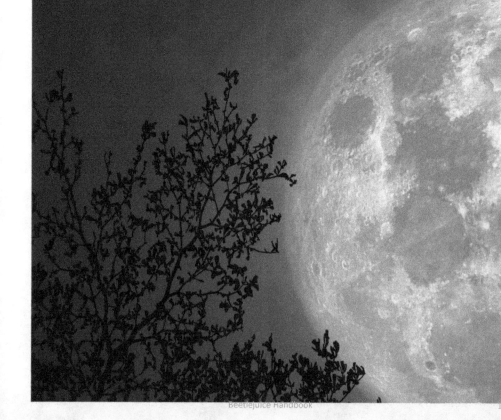

Go ahead,
make my millennium.

Note

Doodle

Note

Doodle

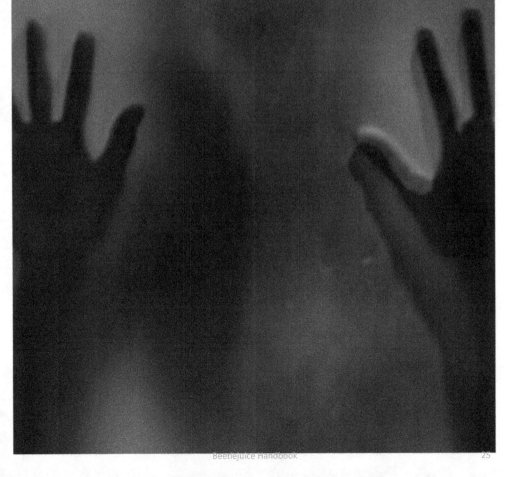

I'm a ghost
with the most, babe.

Note

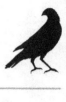

Note

Handbook for the Recently Deceased
Note

Doodle

It's showtime.

— Beetlejuice

Note

Note

Doodle

Note

Doodle

Doodle

Note

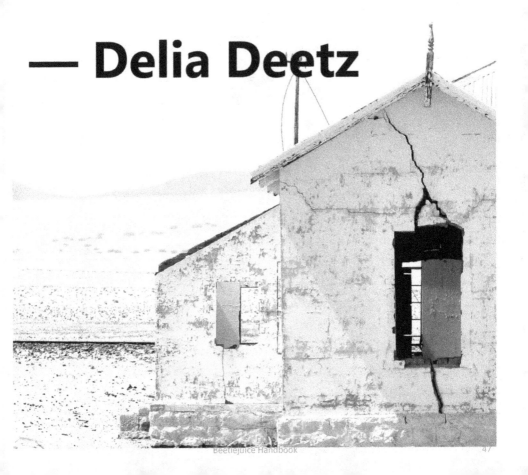

> **"**
> I will live with you
> in this hellhole,
> but I must express
> myself.
>
> — Delia Deetz

Doodle

Note

Doodle

Note

Handbook for the Recently Deceased
Note

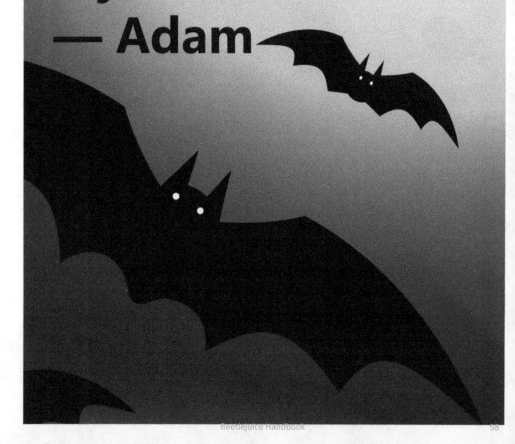

> ## 66
> # We're dead. I don't think we have very much to worry about anymore.
> ## — Adam

Note

Doodle

Note

Doodle

Note

Doodle

Doodle

Note

"Never trust the living!
— Juno

Note

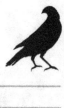

Handbook for the Recently Deceased

Doodle

Doodle

Doodle

Note

Doodle

"
Are you a ghost, too?

— Lydia Deetz

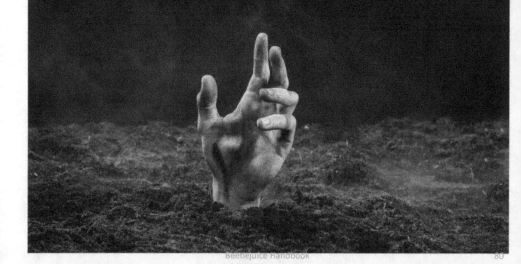

Note

Doodle

Note

Note

Note

Please, they're dead. It's a little late to be neurotic. — Delia Deetz

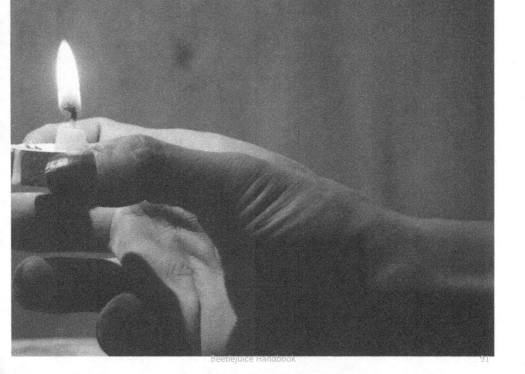

Note

Doodle

Doodle

Note

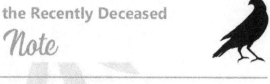

66

What's the good of being a ghost if you can't frighten people away?

— Barbara

Note

Note

Doodle

Note

Thanks

We Congratulate you for taking that
ultimate decision
And buying this Handbook, we hope
you'll achieve
All Your Goals this New Year. You Got
This!
Take out a little of your Time To Rate Us
on Amazon.

Also we appreciate you for believing in
Us and Buying this Handbook. May all
Your Goals Actualize this Year!

CPSIA information can be obtained
at www.ICGtesting.com
Printed in the USA
BVHW030329050821
613541BV00014B/12